Awesome Miracle stories:

THERAPY DOG CASPER

Mary Lee Berger

iUniverse books may be ordered through booksellers or by contacting:

iUniverse
1663 Liberty Drive
Bloomington, IN 47403
www.iuniverse.com
844-349-9409

Because of the dynamic nature of the Internet, any web addresses or links contained in this book may have changed since publication and may no longer be valid. The views expressed in this work are solely those of the author and do not necessarily reflect the views of the publisher, and the publisher hereby disclaims any responsibility for them.

Any people depicted in stock imagery provided by Getty Images are models, and such images are being used for illustrative purposes only. Certain stock imagery © Getty Images.

ISBN: 978-1-6632-3848-1 (sc)
ISBN: 978-1-6632-3849-8 (e)

Library of Congress Control Number: 2022906828

Print information available on the last page.

iUniverse rev. date: 05/06/2022

Casper's business card

CASPER
AUSTRALIAN
LABRADOODLE

Reading Casper's stories you will laugh at his antics, be surprised with his understanding of the English language, be amazed with the decisions he makes on his own, become overwhelmed at his effect on patients and be stunned at how he deals with the death of his patients.

To all the working dogs––past, present, and future
You all are gifts from God. Thank you.

Casper's autograph

kisses and tail wags

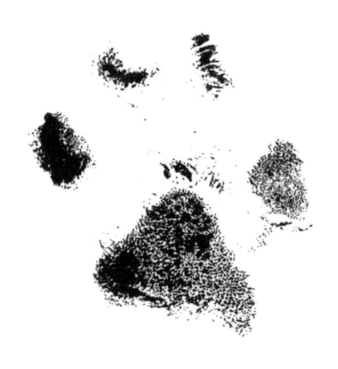

Casper

INTRODUCTION

Casper is a therapy dog. His job is to visit patients to make them feel better.

A service dog is trained many years to work with someone who has a specific problem: seizures, blindness, deafness, etc.

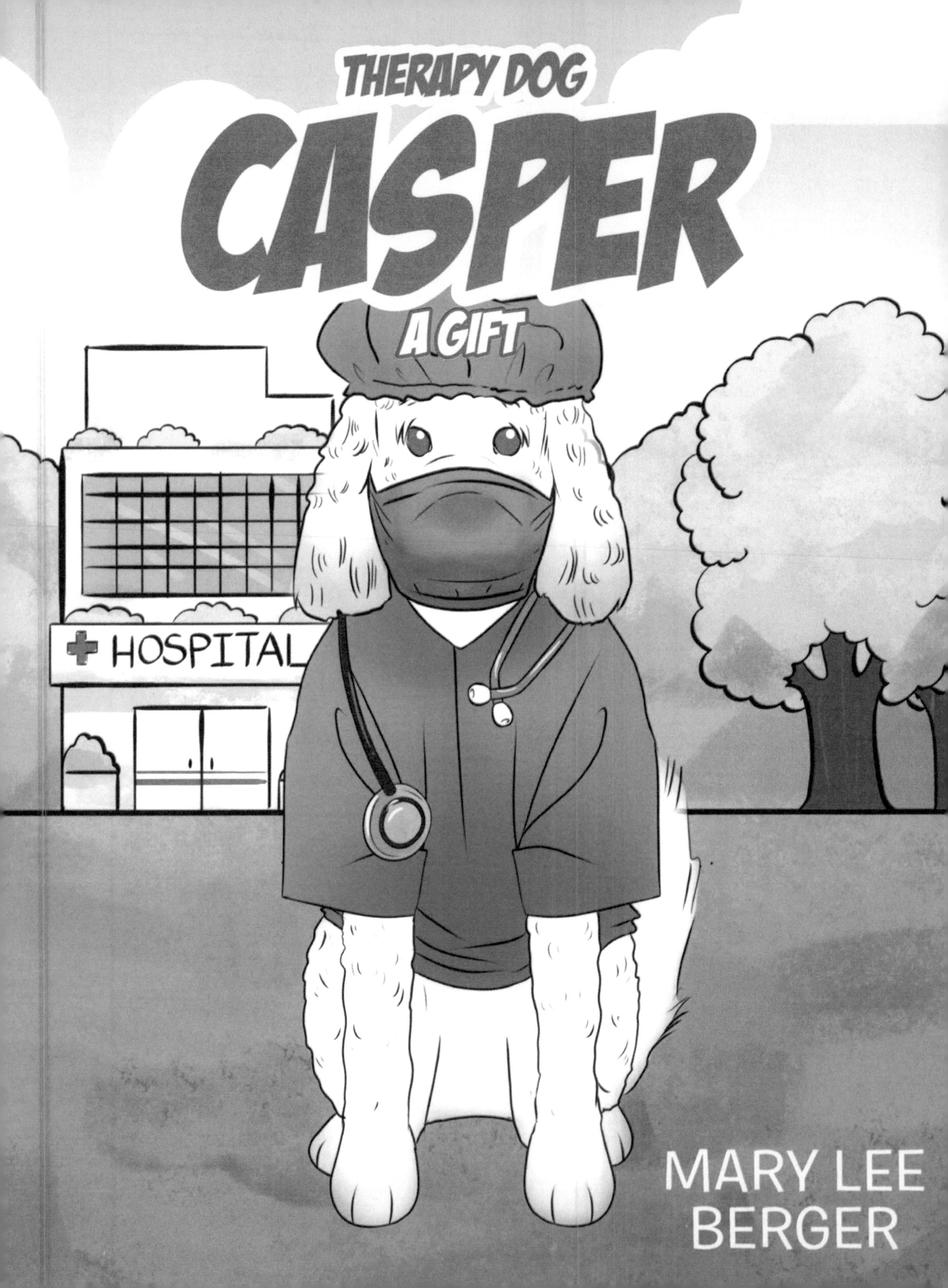
THERAPY DOG
CASPER
A GIFT
HOSPITAL
MARY LEE
BERGER

Casper, a beautiful white Australian labradoodle with big brown eyes that can reach into your soul, came into my life as an eight-week-old puppy. When he reached his first birthday, I started to understand that he was a very special dog.

I wanted him to be a therapy dog but had no information on how to get him started. I saw an announcement for therapy-dog tests. I put him in the car, and off we went to just get information, or so I thought.

On the twenty-minute drive, Casper was acting like any one-year-old puppy, bouncing from window to window and barking at everything he saw. We entered the building with about a dozen other dogs. I noticed that Casper calmed down and immediately his nose went out straight as in a point. His body was like a statue.

The tester came over and introduced herself and said, "Testing would start soon."

I said, "I was just here for information."

She insisted that Casper be tested.

Well he passed with flying colors. The tester remarked that "it was rare for a dog this young to past the test." I did find out that there was a class for therapy dogs, but he did not have to take it since he passed the test.

Our next step was to get registered with a Therapy dog organization. This consisted of paper work and a yearly health exam for him. Next step: find facilities to visit. You cannot walk any dog into a facility and announce you have a therapy dog, and you want to make visits. As his handler, I had to show my Therapy dog credentials, have a background check, a yearly TB test and flu shot. With all this achieved, we were off to visit patients. It slowly became apparent to me that he understood English and what his job was.

MY TOY

One of our first visits was at a nursing home. The patient's walker was by the door. The walker had green tennis balls on the legs. Casper's favorite toys are two green tennis balls. His head went immediately toward the balls. I pulled gently on his leash and gave the command, "Not yours."

He pulled away from the balls with my assurance that his tennis balls were at home. When we arrived home about an hour later, he went to his toy box, pulling out his two green tennis balls, looking up at me, and wagging his tail.

HOLDiNG HANDS

The next visit showed his understanding of the patient's condition. The patient was a frail, little, elderly lady on oxygen. I asked her if she would like a visit from a therapy dog (I always have to ask)?

She said, "Yes."

I walked Casper next to her bed. She reached her arm out but palm up. Casper put his two front feet on the bed and placed a paw in her palm. This brought tears to my eyes as she smiled. I had not yet taught Casper to put his feet up on the bed or much less hold hands/paw. He just knew this lady needed extra love.

OH NO!

Our first visit of significant understanding for Casper came from a visit to our next-door neighbor. Pam and family were from United Kingdom and were here on a work visa.

Pam's twenty-one-year-old son was visiting from United Kingdom. Peter had just graduated from the university with two weeks free time before walking for his diploma. Peter's favorite sport was rugby even though he was much shorter than the average rugby player. This bothered Pam fearing he would be hurt some day.

Peter's father, Mark, drove Peter and his friends to another state to be in a rugby tournament. Pam's fears came true. Peter had a very serious accident, severely damaging his knee. His father brought him home in extreme pain waiting for surgery. Peter was very depressed knowing he would miss his graduation and not knowing if he could play rugby again or just able to walk on that leg.

I asked Pam if a therapy-dog visit would help. She thought it was a good idea. I told her since Casper had been to her house as a friend, I would dress him in his therapy-dog outfit. He is required to wear to health facilities, and likewise, I would wear mine.

We arrived at Pam's house shortly. Casper saw Peter sitting on a large sectional sofa with his leg bandaged and propped up on an ottoman. Casper went over to Peter with his tail wagging.

I said, "Casper, Peter is the patient."

Casper stiffened his body, looked at Peter's bandaged knee, sniffed the air, turned around jumped up on the sofa, curled up as close as he could to Peter, and put his head on Peter's chest.

Pam and I looked at each other with tears in our eyes. Casper does not jump up on sofas at home or away from home. He just knew Peter needed him. At this point, Casper started to make me humble with his actions and understanding. I am glad to say Peter made a perfect recovery and is back in United Kingdom, playing rugby.

THEY JUST KNOW WHAT TO DO

We work at the local hospital every Thursday. We have become friends with the other Thursday volunteers; however, we are the only therapy dog and handler in the group. One of our volunteers had been in failing health for some time and was in and out of the hospital and nursing home. We would visit her where ever she was. She loved Casper so much and was glad to have his visits.

One Wednesday night, another volunteer called me and said our friend was in the hospital and was going to be moved to hospice the next day.

Thursday our regular hospital visiting day. I told her we would get to the hospital as early as we could. We did arrive very early only to learn our friend had passed away a few hours earlier. Our friend had been on the fifth floor where we start our visits. We started our visits and arrived on the fifth floor. We headed to the nurses station to find out which patients would like to have a visit from the therapy dog.

All of a sudden, Casper stopped so abruptly I almost tripped over him. He has never stopped like that in the now two years we have been making therapy visits. He looked into the room he had stopped next to and just stared into the room. He never looks into a room until he knows we are going in for a visit. He stood there and slowly lowered his head for a while. I then realized that the empty, dark room was the room our friend had died in a few hours before.

At this point, I had tears running down my cheeks. I just waited for him to finally raise his head, and he started toward the nurses station to get our visiting assignments. All therapy-dog handlers have a saying, "They just know."

PEACE

While waiting for our daily therapy dog visits at the nurses station in a ICU, I noticed a very frail lady in a room across from us. She was being taken off of life support. I was sad because we had made visits to her. Her daughter saw us and asked if Casper could come in for a visit. I took Casper into the room, he put his two front feet on the bed and scooted up as close as he could get to the patient. He laid his head on the bed looking at her. Her daughter said "Mom, Casper the therapy dog is here to visit with you". With that the patient who was no longer on life support reached out her arm and petted Casper. Yes, we all had tears running down our checks. When she stopped petting him, Casper got down and we went on our way to visit other patients. Down below is the letter the ICU nurse in charge of the patient wrote to the Administration about the incident.

Here is a letter from a nurse in the ICU to the administrator of the hospital.

Dear sir:

It was a busy day in the ICU, I was watching another nurse's patient while she took a patient down for a test. Her patient, I was now watching, was a ninety-seven-year-old lady who had surgery and was now on a ventilator. She was not doing well. Her family decided to make her comfort-care wish. Her family gathered at the bedside as I was making sure her orders were in place, called the chaplain, and made arrangements with respiratory therapy for comfort extubation.

As I was busy getting all these things in place, a family member came out of the room and saw Casper, one of our large white labradoodle therapy dogs. She asked if Casper could come in the room to see the patient, and if Casper could get in the bed with the patient. I paused for a minute and thought about it, given the fact that Casper is not what you would call a lapdog, and the patient was so near the end of her life. But then I asked Casper's handler to bring Casper into the room.

Casper put his front paws on the bed near the patient's hand. The patient began to pet him. Casper began to lick her hand and then got down. The patient seemed to be comforted and at peace.

Her family was very appreciative of Casper's visit and began to express how the patient loved dogs and always had one or two at her house. They began to reminisce about how she had rescued abandoned dogs. There were smiles as the tears began to flow. The patient was extubated shortly after Casper's visit, and she expired about thirty minutes later. Casper's visit gave comfort to a dying patient and her family and turned a difficult situation into a good memory.

From,
Susan B, RN, RNUC in ICU

SANTA PAWS

We were invited to be in the town's Christmas parade with the hospital group. This was Casper's first parade, and he had no idea what to do. Watching the teen girls in front of us running from side to side to the children sitting on the curb giving them candy, Casper got his own idea what he should do. He dragged me from side to side kissing all the children sitting on the curb.

BABY, OH BABY

Casper and I were waiting in a hallway of one of the facilities we visited when a young man with a very newborn in a carrier approached us. He stuck the baby in Casper's face. My heart stopped again. I knew Casper would not hurt the baby, but he had never seen one this young. Casper in his statue stance just looked at the baby, then the baby moved his feet. Casper licked/kissed the baby's feet. The baby started to giggle. Now Casper thinks his job is to lick/kiss all baby feet to make them giggle.

SEEING IS BELIEVING

Some of our stops are at waiting rooms where patients are waiting for tests or procedures. One day, I noticed a woman sitting with her teenage daughter. I asked if they would like to pet the therapy dog. The daughter immediately reached for Casper and started to pet him.

The mother said, "I think you missed what just happened." She said her daughter was having an anxiety attack, and both of her hands were shaking out of control. As soon as she touched Casper, her hands stopped shaking.

The daughter held up her hands which were not shaking. She had a big smile on her face and said, "Thank you."

Just another humbling story.

TWO BY TWO

On one of our visits to the hospital, we met three-year-old twin girls. I could see by the expressions on their faces they wanted to pet Casper, but he is so large they did not know where to try to pet him. Seeing this problem many times, I turn Casper so his side is to the children. I will pet his ears so my hand is between his face and the children. I know he would never hurt a child, but a child could pull his tail, and he might jerk his head around and startle them.

The twins petted him for a long time. When it was time for us to leave, I told the mother, "I was required to offer everyone who petted Casper hand sanitizer." I told her, "I did not want to offer it to the girls without her permission."

She said that was okay; she had hand wipes for them. She gave each girl a wipe and told them, they must wipe their hands because they petted Casper.

They both wiped their hands, and then one girl started to wipe Casper's face. Casper just stood there like a statue. Good boy.

DAD

One day, Casper and I were leaving the ICU floor when I heard footsteps running behind me yelling, "Stop, stop!"

I turned around. There was a middle-aged man. He said his dad had a do-not-resuscitate order. The doctor was standing at the foot of the bed, ready to pronounce the time of death. Could Casper come and visit for a few minutes before the doctor pronounced?

I turned around and went to his father's room. There was the doctor at the foot of the bed and Sue, the nurse from a previous story. Sue said, "Let me put the side of the bed down so Casper can get closer to the patient." She lowered the rail, and Casper, without anything being said, put his two front feet on the bed. He scooted up as close to the patient as he could and laid his head on the man's chest. Casper did this on his own. In a few minutes, Casper got down, and we went on our way.

The next week, we saw Nurse Sue. I said, "Wasn't that amazing what Casper did on his own?"

She said, "What is amazing, the man is alive!"

I said, "What!"

She said, "Look into that room. He is setting up in bed."

I said, "But he was dead when Casper and I went into the room."

She said, "Yes, but when Casper left the man was alive!"

I asked, "How could this be?"

She said, "Some things just cannot be understood."

HE UNDERSTANDS ENGLISH

We were standing at the elevators, waiting to go to the fifth floor to start our visits when a woman ran up to me and asked, "Is your dog a therapy dog?"

I said, "Yes."

She said, "See that woman sitting on the bench crying? She needs a therapy-dog visit."

I went over to the woman, who just reached out her hands, grabbed Casper's head, and buried her face in the long hair on the top of his head. She cried and cried with Casper just standing there like a statue. I sat down next to her and waited for her to stop crying.

When she did, she said, "My husband had a stroke and is not doing well." She then asked, "Can Casper visit him sometime?"

I said, "How about going now?"

We headed up to her husband's room. He was a very large man, and for some reason, his bed was very high up. With Casper's front feet up on the side of the bed, he still could not touch the patient. The wife was standing to my left, and Casper was between us but a little out of my sight.

The wife said, "There is a chair behind me. Do you think we can lift Casper up into the chair and push him up to the bed?"

I said, "Sure, let's try."

We both turned around, and there was Casper sitting in the chair, nose pointing at the patient. We were stunned that he had understood us.

We pushed the chair up to the bed, and Casper started to lick/kiss the patient's hand. Problem understood and solved.

BLESSiNG

In one of the facilities we visit, there is an open area with chairs where patients, mostly with PTSD, are waiting to be called up to a desk to get paperwork. I usually just stand at the side of the group and ask, "Does anyone want to pet a therapy dog?"

This one day, a man literally jumped over a chair to get to Casper. He petted him for a while and then thanked us for being there. We then continued our rounds making our visits and circling around back to the area with the chairs. The same man came up to us and said, "I have been having a bad day until Casper showed up. After you all left, I called my wife on the phone and told her how much better I felt. You may call him Casper, but I call him Blessing."

HE DiD IT AGAiN

Making our rounds one day, we entered a man's room. Out of the corner of my eye, I saw an airborne labradoodle. All of Casper cleared the bed railing. His four feet landed next to the patient, and he was curled up next to him with his head on the patient's shoulder. Of course, my heart stopped for a second because he has never jumped in a patient's bed before. I immediately asked if he was okay, and had Casper hurt him?

The patient said, "I think that Casper's feet never touched me, and he was okay." He just smiled and said, "Dogs just love me." He petted Casper for quite some time with Casper's head remaining on the patient's shoulder.

A nurse I know well came into the room. She had to let the bed rail down so Casper could get out of the bed. Casper just stayed there, not even thinking about getting out of the bed. It took both me and the nurse to pull him out of the bed.

When we got outside of the room, the nurse said, "He did it again!"

I asked, "What did he do?"

She said, "Casper could tell we were moving the patient to hospice in a few minutes."

Yes, more tears running down my cheeks.

UP AND UP

Approaching a patient in a wheelchair, Casper was standing next to him when his arm slipped off the arm of his chair and was just dangling there. The patient looked up at me and said, "I cannot move my arm to pet Casper!"

With that, Casper took one step forward, put his nose under the patient's dangling arm, gave it a hearty flip. The patient's arm went up over his head. Yes, my heart stopped again, wondering where the arm was going to land. As the arm was coming down, Casper took another step forward; the arm came down in the middle of Casper's back. With what little movement the patient had in his fingers, he was able to pet Casper. He looked up at me and smiled. Another problem solved.

SADDEST DAY EVER

In the four years of Casper being a therapy dog, we encountered our saddest day ever. We attended a ceremony called the *last walk*. It was for a military working dog who was retiring because of very poor health. As the TV stations started to set up their equipment, the military lined up along the sidewalk to the vet's office. Several local police K9 officers were in the back, standing at ease behind us with their dogs sitting next to them.

The therapy dogs were next to the vet's door. Casper and I were next to our friend Renice and her dog Cadet. Renice whispered to me, "Have Casper bow when the dog walks past us."

I taught Casper to bow to give patients a little extra love. He stretches his front feet out, head down, and rear in the air. I told Renice, "I was planning on him bowing."

When the retiring dog got in front of us, I gave Casper the command to bow. He did not. Instead he stepped toward her and gave her a kiss from ear to ear. She kissed him back and then walked into the vet's office for the last time. Yes, a flood of tears were running down our faces.

IT IS MINE

In one of the nursing homes we visit, the physical therapy room is next to the front door, making it our first stop of the day. This day, a green plastic ball was rolling across the floor. Casper immediately jumped on it and was chasing it around the room to the patient's delight.

One of the therapists said, "Casper could have the ball because the patients did not use that one."

I said, "I did not want him to take it because I did not want him to think he could shop for toys when we were working."

It took the two of us to pry the ball out of his mouth. Two weeks later when we were back in that PT room, Casper saw the green ball and immediately picked it up. I said to the therapist, "It might be better for him to have the ball so he would not look for it each visit."

He kept it in his mouth for the forty-five minutes while we made our visits. I told the patients he wanted to show off his new toy to them. He still had it in his mouth for the thirty-minute drive home. He only put it down to eat lunch. Then he picked it up and took it upstairs to his bed, and he now sleeps with his special toy.

MAGiC

Stopping at a nurses station to get our visiting assignments, one of the nurses on duty knew Casper well and said "she had a patient with a brain injury who had not responded to anyone since he had been in the hospital". She said, "lets see if Casper can perform his magic". We went into the patients room with two other nurses.

It took them a long time to wake him up. When he opened his eyes you could see that he did not know where he was or what was going on. Our friend said, "you have a special visitor, Casper our therapy dog, can you see him"? His eyes started looking around and finally focused on Casper. The patient then smiled and petted Casper. He also started to talk. The nurses were astonished and said, "that is the first time he has talked"!

Another magical day.

HELP! HELP!

Our house backs up to a navigable creek with a marina across the water, about 200 feet from our house. Last night at midnight with the outdoor temperature at 32 degrees Casper started to bark with an alert bark meaning that something was really in trouble and I needed to check it out. I went to the window did not see or hear anything. Put on the outside lights, still could not see or hear anything. We have a small balcony off of our bedroom, when Casper and I stepped onto the balcony and now David behind us we heard a woman calling for help. I checked with David to make sure he heard the woman also. I suggested that he and Casper stay on the balcony while I went to get the phone and call 911. As I was talking to the 911 operator I stepped back onto the balcony and she could hear the woman calling for help.

Police and fireman arrived on both sides of the water. It took them over an hour to get her out of the water. The dock was to high to get her on the dock so they got a small boat, put her in the boat and rowed here across the creek to our neighbors dock which was lower to the water. They were able to get her onto the dock and then transported to the hospital. She was alive but badly cut by barnacles, and she did live. If Casper had not alerted me I do not believe that woman would be alive today.

I do not think that Casper has ever heard anyone call for help but he knew what to do.

The other amazing part of the story is when I let Casper out first thing in the mourning the first thing he did was to run to the fence and look at the boat the woman had fallen from.

CASPER AWARD THE MAYOR

Casper received his award for saving the woman's life who fell off the boat behind our house, midnight, February 2020 in 32 degree weather.

Everyone in the city knows Casper because of his 6 years of making Therapy dog visits. As we walked into City Hall all the guards rushed over to pet him and said "they had been talking all day that Casper would be here tonight".

We went to Council Chambers and took our seat with others who were receiving awards. The Mayor made rounds bumping elbows with all the award winners. He bumped my elbow than David's. When the Mayor turned around there sat Casper with his right paw up in the air. The Mayor looked at him and then me. I said "he does high fives but I usually have to give him the command". Then the Mayor with a big smile got down on one knee and gave Casper an elbow bump on his raised paw.

I am still amazed at this, Casper has never seen an elbow bump and had to process it as some sort of greeting and then make the decision that he should be a part of this.

THE PHONE RANG

How and where did you get Casper is one of the most asked questions I get. The story is as fascinating as his personal stories. In late June of 2012, the phone rang. It was my friend Leanne a friendship of fifty-plus years. She explained her daughter Linda and twenty of her friends and other family members had booked the first cruise on Disney's new *Fantasy* ship. The reservations had been made eighteen months in advance. She continued that the other grandmother who was to be her cabinmate had just cancelled. Linda had suggested to her mother, Leanne, that she call me and ask if I wanted to take her place. I had always wanted to go on a cruise, but my husband and I never seemed to get around to it, so I jumped at the offer.

I only had a few days to pack and get to Florida because the ship was leaving very soon. Not being a fan of flying, I took the train from Virginia to Florida. The day after I arrived, Leanne and I joined the group and boarded the ship. Leanne and I got separated from the others. While we were trying to find them, a lady came up to us and offered us two extra early boarding passes she had. We gladly accepted and entered the glass elevator heading to our assigned deck. As we looked down, we saw our group looking up at us with astonished looks.

As we arrived to our deck, Leanne looked at me and said, "Oh my gosh, Mary Lee, why do you have tears running down your cheeks?"

The fact that I did have tears running down my face, I said, "Look over there at the white curly dog." I was looking at the back side of this dog who was with a man in a wheelchair. Since he was with the man in a wheelchair, I knew the dog must be a service dog and most likely a labradoodle. I said to Leanne, "I have to have that dog or one like him." I heard the words come out of my mouth, but who really said that? I was shocked at my own words and tears.

As the cruise progressed, we kept running into the dog Rambo and his owner. Each time I would have tears running down my cheeks, Leanne would ask, "Are you really going to get a puppy?"

My answer was always yes! This answer kept surprising me. Who was talking for me? My husband and I had conversations about having another pet but decided, because of our age, a pet could outlive us.

One day after running into Rambo and again the tears running down my cheeks, Leanne asked, "What are you going to name your puppy?"

Without any hesitation or thought, I immediately answered, "Casper!" Casper. Who said that? Where did that come from?

Her next question was somewhat strange: "What are you going to do with him?"

Again without hesitation, I said, "He is going to be a therapy dog!" Again, where did that come from? I never ever thought about having a therapy dog, had no idea how to get one, and what to do with one after I got one.

On the last day of the cruise, we were on the Disney-owned island which was about 110 degrees. We were waiting in line for the tram to take us back to the boat. Leanne looked up at me and saw tears running down my face. She asked, "Now what?"

I said, "Look down. Rambo is licking my fingers. Since he is a service dog, I am not supposed to touch him, and he is a good distance from his owner, which a service dog is never supposed to do." I looked down at him, and I said, "I love you too, Rambo!"

With that, he turned around and went back to his owner.

I had received the name of Rambo's breeder, a breeder of Australian labradoodles in Rockford, Illinois. Upon returning home to Virginia, my husband asked, "How was the cruise?"

To his surprise, I said, "Great, we are getting a puppy!" I called the breeder that day and discovered their puppies were so popular there was a waiting list. I placed my name on the list; this was early July 2012. Casper was born November 11, 2012. He arrived at his new home in Virginia in late January 2013. So it all began with an unexpected phone call.

CASPER'S PHOTO ALBUM
OUTFITS FOR SPECIAL OCCASIONS

HALLOWEEN AT THE HOSPiTAL

HAPPY VALENTINES DAY

CASPER SAFELY LEADING
THE NEIGHBORHOOD
CHILDREN IN THEIR HALLOWEEN PARADE

MERRY CHRISTMAS

HAPPY EASTER

HAPPY 4TH OF JULY

SPECIAL TREAT FOR
WORKING A LONG DAY

HAPPY THANKSGIVING

ABOUT THE AUTHOR

Mary Lee Berger has had a very exciting life, moving fifty times and attending nineteen different schools. Her degree was in interior design and then added real estate broker. Living in the Washington, DC, area, she was able to work with celebrities and politicians.

One of the most adventurous times of her life was selling their house and moving to and living on their boat for over five years. She has been married to her husband, David, for over fifty years. They are parents of identical twin boys.

She has had many pets in her life––from dogs, cats, rabbits, ducks, pigs, and chickens––but nothing prepared her for the extraordinary insight and unexplainable powers of Casper, her therapy dog.

Printed in the United States
by Baker & Taylor Publisher Services